M I C R O G R A M S

❀

MICROGRAMS

❀

NICOLE
WALKER

NEW MICHIGAN PRESS
TUCSON, ARIZONA

NEW MICHIGAN PRESS

DEPT OF ENGLISH, P. O. BOX 210067

UNIVERSITY OF ARIZONA

TUCSON, AZ 85721-0067

<http://newmichiganpress.com>

Orders and queries to <nmp@thediagram.com>.

ISBN 978-1-934832-54-7. FIRST PRINTING.

Printed in the United States of America.

Design by Ander Monson.

Cover photo © Buccaneer | Dreamstime.com -
Fern Prothallium (prothallus) Photo

CONTENTS

MICROBARRIERS

Inside the human organism live two hundred species of microorganisms. Different strains of each species multiply. A human, standing on a scale, weighs as much in micro as she does in macro, if you count the weight of the dust mite and the weight of the digestive enzyme. But these gut microorganisms represent the diversity and colonizing-power of the human-bacteria relationship. The small intestine, unrolled and split open like an earthworm under the microscope, spans the area of a flayed blue whale—the largest organism on the planet. Inside the flayed whale you could find as many species of microorganisms in the whale's intestine as inside the human's. Flayed, both whale and human intestine span an area large enough to park seven school buses.

Inside the seven school buses you can fit forty-seven children, each with his or her own histrionic number of microorganisms, which, in the mind of a first grader, look like little earthworms. If you want to get someone to eat an earthworm, try a first grader, who will eat anything baked in brown sugar that reminds him or her of a gummy worm. You can tell a baked-in-brown-sugar earthworm from a gummy worm by the way, when you flay them, a million kinds of microorganisms spill out.

Where the human starts and the world begins is determined inside the gut. The microorganisms perform a border. Although they are the world inside you they also protect you from the world, and, truly, from themselves. The gut microbes make a barrier between you and the outside world, although they, outers, are also inners. They are a paradox, these microbes. The microorganism can try to kill you if his name is *Clostridium botulinum* but your friend, *Bifidobacterium*, can keep him from completing his mission. Lactobacilli fights *E. Coli* everyday. Imagine a million Greek soldiers in the horse that is your gut. You are together in this fight, *Bifido* and horse, whale and lactobacilli.

When the world was not of you, you were not always of this world. Not until you journeyed through your mother's birth canal, did the previously non-organismed inside of your body become colonized with bacteria. The vaginal canal and its microorganisms infected you. And now you are safely infected with the world. Inside out, you thank the barrier for keeping in check the salmonella. You thank the bacteria for holding back the proliferation of viruses, microorganisms even

protection thru infection

go thru *much* to join the human community

anthropomorphism
growing up—breaking barriers

smaller than bacteria that are just using you like the bad boyfriend you had in 9th grade for your willingness to replicate and host another species in your body. At least bacteria have mutual respect for one another. Viruses bring nothing to the table. They don't even open the car door for you. They just line the passenger side seat with condoms they pretend to wear.

The gut barrier, like a good condom, keeps bad bacteria out. The good bacteria neutralize bad if they get in. I read today about a shooting inside the parliament building in Canada, a two-year old dying from the Ebola virus outside a hospital, a soldier joining the Kurdish Army inside Iraq, a Voter ID law approved in Texas, an shelf sloughing off ice into a cold but warming sea, a deer, foot caught in a fence, dying trying to get it out. I do not want these words inside me but my ears do not serve as a barrier device. My eyes do not act as a barrier device. My forehead does not act as a barrier device. My skull does not act as a barrier device. My brain, perhaps if had been raised on yogurt's probiotic features, could act as a barrier device, but alas, alack, this brain has no way to keep the outside out. She apologizes, this inside brain, for doing a bad job of keeping the inside in. One day, they (we) will invent microorganisms to protect the brain from itself.

overwhelmed
onslaught
porous

good bacteria
oxymoron

*Who is this "you"?
docs it change??*

MICROMEAT

If you're going to eat meat, you should buy the meat locally. If you're going to eat meat, you should make sure the animal didn't suffer in a small box or a large box or shit in a lagoon or spend its life trampling over streams, destroying salmon spawning grounds, or be shipped from one side of the country in a boxcar with open-air panels or shipped back in a refrigerated semi-truck. If you're going to eat meat, you shouldn't shove the meat full of antibiotics so that you're conspiring to help the superbugs become resistant to antibiotics. You shouldn't hobble the animal as its put on the conveyer belt toward the ends of its life. You shouldn't daze the animal with drugs or stun guns before you slit its throat.

If you're going to eat meat, you should buy the meat locally. So local that it might mean homegrown. So local that you raised four goats in the backyard and let the goats have sex and get pregnant and have tiny goat babies that you fed from a bottle. But, if you're going to eat meat, so locally, you shouldn't count the babies.

artisanal
Portlandia send up

You shouldn't name the babies. You shouldn't or maybe
you should, introduce your children to the goats. You
shouldn't, or maybe you should, let your children watch
as you whet the knife against the stone you couldn't find
locally so you bought through Amazon.com.

You should invite your friends over, especially the
ones who read *The Iliad* with you at Reed College. You
should remember how hungry that book made you. A
roasted goat. The beginning of Western Civilization.
You should make an offering to your household gods.
You should try to think of this as an offering—to the
CAFO cows, to the sweet neighbors who don't complain
about the smell, to the truck drivers who didn't have
to drive this goat to you, to the mother of this goat
and the mother of your child, to your child who you
couldn't decide whether or not to let watch and so you
do because knives are decisive and goats are small but
this one has big eyes into which you are trying not to
look, into which you are trying to erase as you've erased
so many cows' eyes in the past. You don't look at your
daughter's eyes either. You look at the fur on the throat.
You try to think of it as a wool blanket. You've seen
wool blankets spun before your eyes before. You can
part that weave. You should be able to part this one. For
the first time, you know the pleasure of pre-wrapped
meat. You would give anything for the protective film
of plastic right now. A little black foam. Oh steak. Oh
Safeway, you think as you do something you have no

again,
painter,
between
pet + meal

"kid"
duality

"clean"
sterile
no back story, no mess

training for, as your friends, those who read *The Iliad* turn away and only your wife holds the feet and only you drag the blade across the throat and only you hand the baby goat upside down to let the blood drain out like you read you were supposed to on Wikipedia.

You build a fire. You dig a pit. Into the pit you bury the dead baby goat. You layer oregano and lemons on top. Sprinkle salt. You put coals on top of the meat and let it roast like any good Achaean. The smell of smoking meat brings the friends back. It brings the neighbors over. Someone said they could smell the smoke all the way down the street at Reed College. The goat, cooked, is unlike anything you've ever tasted. The goat is all the meat you've ever wanted.

The next year, when the baby goats are born, you dig into your pockets, find a twenty dollar bill and take it to Safeway to celebrate new life.

back to our roots—but we can't entirely (internet age) compartment-alization

community

conscience costs

MICROSCOPIUM

In the 1968 film, *Powers of Ten*, Charles and Ray
Eames adjust the lenses of their cameras and zoom
out. Beginning with a man at a picnic in a park, every
ten seconds, then one meter wide, viewed one meter
away, every 10 seconds the lens moves 10 times farther
away and the field of view grows ten times wide. Cars.
Docks. 1,000 meters. City on the lake shore. Edge of
Lake Michigan. Then the whole lake. 10 to the 6th earth
as solid sphere. Then, whole earth. Good night moon.
Paths of planets: Venus, Mars, then Mercury.
    Then, that sun, causing its imposing light all over.
But then everything disappears to black with speckles,
an enamel canning pot. Oh universe. How did you grow
so small?

*

On Sunday night, a student from a class I taught just
last year, Jordan, age 21, was riding her bicycle through a

how do we demarcate "neighborhood"

collision
Big Bang
single death

neighborhood south of the school when another 21 year old drove her F150 drunk, 66 miles per hour, through that neighborhood. A neighborhood is only as big as the streets are wide, as the reflectors are bright, as the sidewalks are thick, as the stop signs are red. This was a small neighborhood. So small that a driver, driving fast, can't even see that it's not a freeway, it's a neighborhood. The driver, driving fast, drunk, exponentially, shifts into the ten to the seventh power and then, there is no bicycle. Then, there is no girl with hair as black as the paint on your truck, as black as your skid marks as black as the sky beyond the reach of the sun.

That is the problem with death. In the zooming of both time and space, you become smaller and smaller. Now, you're a picture on the cover of the Arizona Daily Sun, a newspaper so small that the crease is as thin as a cut and thereby, you are halved again.

*

And then we pause and start back home. This emptiness is normal. The richness of our own neighborhood is unique. Let's go home. Let's get away from this dangerous universe. Let's look inside instead. Two seconds per exponent this time. 10 to the 7th, 6th, 5, 4, 3, 2, 1. Let's reduce. Let's go smaller. 10 to the -2, approach the surface of the man on the picnic, cross layers of the skin, tiny blood vessels, an outer layer of cells, a capillary

opposites, extremes
Big to Small, grow/shrink

containing red blood cells, then into nucleus of the
man, holding the heredity of the man, the coiled DNA
itself, in an alphabet of 4 letters, the code for the man, 4
electrons. Quantum motion. At 10 to the minus ten. We
enter a vast inner space. The carbon nucleus. So large
and so small. The domain of universal modules. A single
proton fills our screen, fuels our scene.

*

Jordan is still full of potential energy. Jordan's carbon
atoms still dot the curb. Those protons still shimmer
with the quantum energy. If only we could get to know
Jordan again, at this quantum level. A class held on the
side of the road, her words as inky as ten to the 40th
power, her words as resonant as the hydrogen bonds
that keep the street, the grass, the tire, the bumper,
the metal, the thump, the braking, braking, braking all
together.

we're
"bound"
together

pun-break

MICROSURGERY

They still used a saw to cut off my grandma's leg.
It's circular now in the twenty-first century but the
chiseling teeth are a quarter of an inch long and curved
as a scythe. I imagine something so much softer, a
pink eraser from grade school that just gently removes,
rolling pencil off paper cleanly, if not wholly.

One of the first hard scenes in a movie I saw—I'd like to
think it was Oscar winning *Das Boot* auf Deutsch but
was probably just the Sunday night movie I was allowed
to stay up just to hang out with my parents, (I was the
oldest and therefore, thought mature)—a man lay in
the bottom of a life boat and his companions handed
him a knife to bite down on as they cleanly and wholly
removed his leg.

When my sister found out they had to remove my
grandmother's gangrenous leg, she said, "Don't worry
grandma, I'll get you a bullet to bite on," and "Well, now
you won't have to dress up for Pirate's Day anymore." I

wished I could have made my grandma laugh instead
of crying and making pointless circles motions with my
hands.

How old do you have to be for the vascular surgeons
to give up? At 85, their microtools lay on the bottom of
a lifeboat, unmovable for all the waves of diabetes and
knots of veins. At 65, they might take the microscope to
a vein, see how much shaking hand the cell walls could
tolerate. At 50, they'd most probably go in. You have
good proteins, good platelets and a steady line of health
insurance. At 40, they're banging to get in those veins of
yours,—hello, I'm a pirate, they say. I've come to practice
on your relatively soft and pliable capillaries with my
microhook and microsails.

[handwritten marginalia: telescopic zoom in & out modern, techno. writing for our age]

But at 85, my grandmother lies in her hospital bed with
a foot as rotten as any German film. Her leg does not
pulse like it did in elementary school, or in high school
or when she got married the third or the fourth time,
or when she gave birth to my mother, sixty miles from
home in the town of Coalville where they let her stay in
bed for a week. She luxuriated in every moment of that
hospital stay—the one where her daughter came early
but breathed on her own, where her nurses wouldn't let
her get out of bed, instead brought her every meal, 1, 2,
3, even sometimes 4 a day. She loved that hospital, the
hospital she knew she would be on two feet to walk out
of.

[handwritten marginalia: give women a break aging, viability handicapped piracy]

MICROENCEPHALY

When Zoe was almost two, her pediatrician made
her have an MRI to see what kind of encephaly was
happening inside her head. How much foot down
can you put when the doctor measures her head
circumference to be a hundred and ten percent of
normal? Can you say, "I know she's fine," even though
you know she's fine without sounding like you doth
protest too much? What if you're wrong (even though
you know you're not) and her brain pushes against the
already-large circumference of a skull like a flooding
river against a high-built dam? So you give in and
let them lie her down on the table. You let them put
the cotton balls on her eyes. You let them fire up the
magnets and let rays batter against her head like the sun
batters against the planet and look what you get? An
image of the world all inside her head. Birds sheltering
squirrels hiding under owls inside trees cutting out
canoes on top of fjords shadowing granite slab and then
flower burst after flower burst inside of which of course

little kid lang.

mother knows best

mother doll, protection

seed then lettuce then tomato a whole salad for a brain.
The world is best protected nestled inside itself like
Matryoshka dolls and her head is big, yes, but also large,
and expansive and if there's anyone I would entrust, and
I mean "en" to read "in," it is my large headed daughter
who woke up from the anesthesia and wanted to go get
chicken for dinner because of all the birds in her heads.

chicken, egg

    I try not to blame myself: My son and husband also
host huge heads. They make fun of me for my smaller-
sized head which I say is not that small and I tease them
back saying I hope you don't tip over, top-heavy, planet-
sized-head-riddled babies. I put hat upon hat upon
them and they never do fit. A house full of big heads
and an overly permissive parent (small, unimaginative
brain that couldn't foresee sickness, danger, death) who
lets her kids play hatless in the snow.

contrast btwn little girl, big issue

birdbrain

MICROLECITHAL

You were in Nancy's class, not mine. I only saw you
because you were in the writing center and I was in the
writing center although I don't write there all that much.
You were wearing not quite a burka but your head was
swaddled and your dress was a robe, trailing the floor. In
the desert, the robe makes some sense—it keeps the sun
from burning pale skin. The long hem of the skirt skims
sand, rushes air up, underneath. On that side of the
world pointing fat side to the sun, long and covered yet
light and breezy makes sense. The headscarf translates
well to Flagstaff weather. In the winter, you want to
keep your head covered, especially in the morning when
the temperature blips between plus one and minus one,
plus one and minus one. But those skirts drag in the
snow. The edges soak. Melted snow inches up the robe.
All day long, you become wet in a way you fear might
offend Mohammed.

You hadn't felt the baby kick for three days. You are
eight months pregnant on the other side of the world

from home and you do not know what this means. This is your first baby. You came here because the Center for International Education invited your husband, and your husband invited you. You are a student of English and yet the word "kick" doesn't translate here. You wonder if it's the cold that's slowing the baby down. You wonder if it is the thin air here. You wonder if it is the way the earth contracts away from the sun, this far north, at this elevation, like a Gap girl tightening the belt on her low-cut jeans. Nancy asks me if it is normal for babies to be so quiet for three days. I say, sometimes, when it's warm, the baby doesn't move. But I don't know what I'm talking about. When I was pregnant I was cold all the time and the baby came early—before the eight months pregnant you are.

Later that day, you sent Nancy an email. You had gone to the health center as Nancy had suggested. At the health center, in a language you were studying but couldn't quite say was your own, you heard the nurse practitioner tell you that the baby had died. Inside, as you had walked through snow, the baby was already sloughing off cells. The baby was already decomposing under that veil of dress and skin. Under that skin, *Matryoshka* the baby that had made the skirts billow forth, the stomach that had made its own equator collapsed and contracted. The baby that you had been trying to be hold up fell down. You couldn't tell your husband, any more than you could tell your mother, that it was the baby who had kept you gravitationally erect. Now, baby-shrinking, head collapsing, skin-sloughing, your skirts weighed more than the sun itself. The equator shrank. You slipped across the now-flat of the world as if upon ice.

re-Orientation

lost gravity

meterological phenomenon weather systems in- external climates

MICROBORTION 1

People always bring up math. A million fish in the
sea. One million sperm, flushed. One million people
starving somewhere near my backyard but not in it. One
in a million possibilities—a green bird with a yellow
beak. A pumpkin with a face cut into it. A girl playing
basketball as the sun splashes into the sea. And then
they take it down a notch. One in 1,000. One in 100.
One in ten chances and nobody will cover the odds. At
twenty weeks they saw something. At twenty weeks
the bend in the spine, the crook of the neck, the shape
of the nose, too many signs to add up to human. This
imprint of a child who had not yet twisted her head
toward breast, who knew only the stuff of fish—water,
bob, gases, flip—came pre-broken. The world wouldn't
have its chance to do its worst to her. The only thing
now was to wait—wait for the twenty more weeks, wait
for the gasp or air, wait for the ventilator, wait for the
mask, wait for the paralytics that kept her fins from
flapping against herself, bruising her forehead, bluing

the
short,
blunt
cut
wallop end

her cheeks. The mother had always loved fish. She
would spend her life regretting the ocean.

↳ why? source of
abnormality (wives' tales?)

afterthought
shame, inconspic,

MICROBORTION 2

It attached to her uterus like a wad of gum under a
table. It ballooned inside of her until her insides were
more peppermint than blood. When she finally made
it to the doctor, it was too late to remove the growth.
18 weeks was the limit and even God could see she was
pregnant now. At week 40, she tried to dislodge that
wad with the force of a chisel. As the doctors tugged
on the head, they pulled the woman inside out, turning
her and the matter of her birth sticky. Now, at the
playground, she's stuck to the bench, stuck on her ass,
stuck drinking Tab, smacking gum against gum against
gum.

young girl

gummy pun toothless
youth "popped" short
lost its flavor

MICROBORTION 3

She loved the baby already just like she loved otters.
She loved the baby already just like she loved the swell
of her breasts, the frog of her belly, the clanking of her
widening hips. But this baby couldn't be hers. Twelve
years old. She loved otters. That's why she let them
swim in the sea.

let it be free
—similar to MB#1

MICROBORTION 4

She would pay for it. That's what they always told her.
She would pay. And, since he wouldn't pay, she did pay,
or tried to. She worked for tips. She sold her books.
She gave someone a blowjob for $25. She'd given them
for more, for less, in the past. She added up the cash.
She took it to the clinic. The clinic told her to keep her
money. She'd need it for diapers. She took the money.
She handed it to the he. Then, she reached up inside her
vagina and gave the he the uterus, the fallopian tubes,
the amniotic sac. She'd given more for less, before. As
she lay on the floor, her sweater absorbing the blood,
she remembered one good thing. But then it slipped
away before she could grab hold of it. It didn't matter,
anymore, anyway. Not like the handful of blood. That
meant something. It meant all the world to the he as he
held the throbbing of it in his inexpensive hands.

MICROBORTION 5

Enough should be enough. The children were like barnacles. Multiplying. Sticky. She got pregnant every time she sneezed. As if she was in charge of dust in her nose. As if she were in charge of the sun in her eyes. As if she were the she here was in charge of the putting it in. No. She was just in charge of the taking it out. So she took them out. Sometimes full term. Sometimes preterm. But the boat. It was getting heavy. It was starting to sink. The men saw her. Instead of sticking their hands out to help her up, they stuck their dicks in her. They sat on her. They pushed her down, holding onto her shoulders. And then she went under. As the last air from her lungs (no one else's) pushed bubbles into their world, she wished she'd been fitted with a man guard, a chastity belt, a vagina that was part piranha. But instead, she'd been fitted with a working uterus, luscious lips, and a bad habit of forgetting to vote.

[handwritten margin notes: "self-other strong-weak", "triplicat hit →", "what does it mean to be a woman"]

MICROBLADDER

No one likes the movie *Waterworld*. My friends Ander
and Megan bought me a copy of a board game based on
Waterworld but no one will play it with me. The logic
is too squirrely—why do the smokers have so much
gasoline? Why so many cigarettes these many years later
after the continents have all been swamped? In what
Natural Selection game can you turn fish in a few short
generations Kevin Costner needs lime but he has gills?
Darwin would not play *Waterworld* either.

*

My sister and I traveled to New York City together.
Before he died, my dad liked to take us on vacations—
airplane or rented RV or sometimes boat and often
NYC. This was the first time my sister and I traveled
alone together. People kept giving us free things—a
hundred bucks off a three-hundred dollar sushi dinner
bill. We ate quivery urchin and fatty tuna back when

tuna was fat, a bottle of wine as we exited the shared cab, and, finally, two free beers a piece in the afternoon before we our flight left for home.

On the way to the airport, as we drove through Queens, I lay down on the backseat of the town car. I squeezed my sister's hand. She was trying to defuse the pain. A bladder full of two Heineken. If we had been near home, I would have asked to stop, but nothing feels as foreign as the backseat of a Lincoln on the expressway, car abutting car, heading toward JFK with a bladder full of beer.

*

Still, I like the movie— the way I cannot go there. I cannot travel to *Waterworld*. It doesn't exist. There is no travel opportunity missing. There is no thing I can own. Water, malleable, moving, Protean, resists possession.

capitalism

*

I took yet another plane, not even bothering to offset my carbon output by buying carbon credits, to Hawaii. This time, it was all of us: My sister, her husband, her son, my mom, her boyfriend Tom, my husband and his parents. 9 of us on an airplane. We each used 1.6 tons of carbon to get there. (We could have bought our consciences clean at air travel offset dot com for $208.03.

We didn't.) Perhaps we could have driven to California where they also have beaches.

But instead, we went to Kailua and watched the volcano pour enough lava onto hot ground to make us think the world had enough hot stuff to power itself.

Later, we realized we would need snorkeling gear and that snorkeling gear was cheaper to buy than rent. We drove both rental cars to Walmart. I refused to go in. I boycott Walmart for all the reasons there are to boycott Walmart. I waited in the car. At least until I had to pee. I didn't think peeing at Walmart would infringe on my no-Walmart policy. I tried to pee on the floor a little, to let Walmart know just what I thought about them. I didn't buy anything there. I wouldn't even look around but it was thanks to Walmart gear, the snorkel mask in particular, imported from China, that I saw that giant sea turtle swimming away from me. Thank you, Walmart. Thank you, China.

out of sight, mind

vacationing from life

moral fiscal gray area

*

I take comfort in *Waterworld*'s metaphor that there is a destination like dry land. Dry land is the thing opposite what you already have. It's the dream of finding abundance through scarcity. A lime tree in the middle of the ocean makes you love lime more than water. Dry land, just a block of it, if you could find it, would give you everything you need. It would serve all the earth

26

for your individual human needs. You could find an old car. Go driving around the top, which must be, in some way, Mt. Everest. You could take comfort in the fact that if you spit or piss on or exhaust it enough, that it will remind you of home and that you can stay on this new land that looks a lot like old land for as long as the water stops rising.

make
mark

global
warming
Darwinism
(de)evolution

MICROBURSTS

1.

The ravens fly low through the trees. I believe they want
a little of my hair. Like X-wing fighters, they seem to be
targeting my head. They must think that I am water or
at least a source thereof, or perhaps I'm just in their way,
drinking my mason jar full of ice. I leave the jar outside
sometimes. Maybe they'll take the bait.

2.

I shouldn't yell I shouldn't yell I shouldn't yell but why
in God's name can't you wear other shoes. No two-year
old should be so adamant about wearing flip flops. I
don't mean to lift you up hard and put you down in your
crib soft but I didn't even say no, I just suggested that
possibly, you might want to wear other shoes to play
soccer or baseball or run outside without getting sand

and rocks stuck in your sandals. You sit down in the dirt, getting your pants as dirty as your soles and take off your flip flops every sixteen seconds to wipe off the sand and the rocks and then you put the flip flops back on and run and trip and cry and blame me for letting you wear those stupid shoes.

3.

I got caught out. My hair is stupid, swiveled upward by wind. My skirt, drenched. You think the clouds are just teasing you but they are as big of assholes as I am. They wander by, you beg them for rain, they blow out of town without even letting loose one drop. And then the next thing you know, you and your computer and your book are outside. It looks pretty clear, except for that one cloud. You type a sentence, copy a passage, drink from your Mason jar. And then out of nowhere, you are swimming in your own stew, a combination of misplaced trust and self-deprecation. You would run from this downpour but you've been asking for it, you know. Plus, you too, who were insistent on dumb shoes, cannot run away from this storm in flip-flops.

big little
dumb
at nature's mercy

MICRO PRAIRIE DOGS AND MICRO TURKEY VULTURES

70 days it hasn't rained. It's a record but when I turn
on my tap, the water still runs. On the drive home
from Kayenta, horses were licking the side of the road,
hoping whatever had spilled from that Ford F150 ahead
spilled something lappable.

Nearer to my house, the prairie dogs run into the
road. My daughter Zoe screams when she sees them
on the yellow lines. They pile upon the stripes, for
some reason. Perhaps they think, as I do, that massing
together brings rain. Maybe they're trying to cover
up the yellow that is obviously preventing the black
monsoon clouds from letting go their water. Maybe they
are trying to get to the other side, where the houses have
hoses. The yellow lines bar them from access.

I should bring a bowl of water to them, although that
may be somewhat like littering—big pink bowl in the
middle of the prairie dog town. And I'm no scientist.
I shouldn't interfere with their ecosystem. And yet, I
already am sucking up all their water through my pipes.

I water the daisies with them. Daisies from Mt. Shasta who somehow think this desert-living isn't so bad, as long as you have a Nicole to tend to you.

I still might take the water to the prairie dogs just like I still might take the chicken drumsticks that have gone bad in my refrigerator out into the woods for the vultures. I worry that the vultures might get salmonella but I'm pretty sure their stomachs are prepared for rotten chicken. I worry more that they may become reliant on my chicken delivery service and next week will start amassing on the fence. I'll try to go running through the gate with my dog and they, sensing no chicken, will find Nicole meat tasty enough. Or they'll at least look at me with their turkey necks. Chicken-loving cannibals. So instead I throw the chicken in the garbage. Five chickens died for those ten legs. And now the vultures are hungry and the prairie dogs are thirsty and so I have a glass of wine, and save some water, turn away from the forest, turn away from the prairie dog town, look at the sunset, look out to sea wondering if this is the kind of world that will remember to bring water out here.

MICRO SNOW LEOPARD

Noun: 1. Ounce. 2. noun snow leopard.
Origin: 1300–50; Middle English unce: lynx,
French: Old French: once, variant of lonce
(erroneously taken as *l'once*, the ounce)

I don't know how it happened. I was reading online
about snow leopards and how they're losing habitat,
and, now worse, the treeline, the actual place where
trees can grow is moving up, thanks to you-know-who
(Voldemort, Global warming), are moving up. The snow
leopard finds the heavy fact of trees non-negotiable.
The snow leopard prefers the liminal space of snow and
sky. Snow leopards have been on the verge of extinction
since Peter Matthiessen's great book where he tracks
the snow leopard through the Himalayas where he
meets many lamas, where he never sees a snow leopard.
A whole book of never finding. A whole world of too
much finding. While I'm reading, I'm also looking up
micro words, as I do every day. I clicked twice. Once on

meditationn
obsession
soothing

snow leopard, once on dictionary.com. And the lynx,
another name for snow leopard somehow shows up
under ounce. How we pronounce our deaths. No one
can take it all at once. A draught of tar a day. An aspirin
an hour. A sip of petrochlorate in the water. I am done.
I am done, I say every day. I do not think I can do this
any longer. This living slow. This slow dying. This world
squeezes out snow or leopards ounce by ounce. The
snow leopard, unfound by Peter Matthiessen, does not
exist already. He is a figment, smaller than an ounce.
He moves as treelines move— through hair, and ounce,
and lynx and shift. If no one bothered looking, he'd be
safely splitting the difference between ouns and unce.
He'd be throating the vowels. Coughing up the narrow
split. He'd be middle English, middle passage, middle
aged. He'd be done, he'd say every day. Done lynx. Done
ounce.

MICROHABITAT

A tree, fallen in the forest, turns to hair. What is the purpose of hair? To keep germs out of the nose. To keep grains of sand out of the eyes. To keep the head warm when the snow piles on, when the winter begins to think everything is dead and ready to be reinvested, recycled, reincarnated in the dirt. But not everything is dead on the hair. Dust mites, even on the dead, still clean the eyelashes. The nasal cilia cling to the inside of nose. The roots of cold hair turn colder under snow.

The tree, though fallen, isn't dead. I have seen, on the hairs of the decomposing tree, a banana slug the length of my arm, scratching its underbelly against grain. In its slimy path, a microbe nestles. It is fed by the slime. It respires the hairs of the fallen the tree, turning the hair to hummus, opening the chemical strand to let new carbon in. Deep inside the fallen tree, under the hair, the carbon cycles. It looks for its rhizome partner. The rhizome has been waiting for this little death for two-hundred and twenty-three years. Tickled by the carbon, the rhizome swells, breaks through stiff hair. The mushroom rises up, engorged. Its spores search for wind. The wind, carrying spores and oxygen to vie for space with all this decomposing carbon, brings its own reformation. It streams through the hairs, parting them, open space for the seed from the pinecone to lodge. Inside its old tree, under the warmth of a tropical slug, beside a lascivious rhizome, surrounded by the microbe-pulsing hummus, the seed of the Douglas Fir stretches out its cilia in the skeleton of forest. Its sprout clings to a tendril of hair. The hair hoists the sprout. The sprout. The first hair. The next tree.

NEUTRINOS

When I was fifteen, I read a book about a mute girl who
went to a bar to see a show. She went into the bathroom
and came out with the lead singer's name carved into
her forehead. The lead singer, guilty and guilted,
married the girl. It wasn't until after the wedding, after
the baby, after the years of silence does the lead singer,
who doesn't sing anymore, discover it was not his wife
who cut his name in her forehead. A stranger-woman
accosted his now-wife in the bathroom and carved his
name in her forehead. Should he have married that
woman instead?

Neutrinos could tell us but neutrinos, in their
mathematic existence, don't talk. If the universe is
indeed expanding, then, we will surely never die. Of
course, we get the news too late. Dead stars sending
obituaries of light. The name reads backwards in the
mirror. We can't see our future until it's very well past.

—

I Googled this: "Cesar girl carved name bathroom singer." Google came back with a different book, one by Anne Tyler about a different girl who carved the name of a singer she had a crush on into her forehead. It is not the same book. My book had a woodcut of the word "Cesar" on the cover. But Google already knows what I was going to ask. It already came up with a close-enough answer. No wonder no one reads books anymore.

It is very difficult to observe neutrinos, especially muon and tau neutrinos. First you must know neutrons, electrons and protons. Then you must know anti-neutrinos. Invite them over for video games. Once you have gotten to know them, try to steal the joystick. The way the hand goes slack. The speed of resignation. You now have all the control in your hands. And now you know something else about the universe. Neutrinos are weak.

The book, not my book but Anne Tyler's, is now also a movie starring Guy Pearce. I can't picture Guy Pearce but I think of Pierce Brosnan who played Remington Steele about the same time as I read my book about the girl who carved/was carved names of future husbands that she really did not necessarily already love.

—

There are so many neutrinos in the universe that even
a small neutrino mass can display great significance.
Think of the Grand Canyon. Think of a piece of sand.
Think of a piece of sand falling into the Grand Canyon,
into the river. Weigh the Colorado. How do you
measure absence? What did moving that grain of sand
dislodge? How did it lose itself in its fall? According
to Edward Wright of UCLA, "The energy spectrum
of the observable electrons in a radioactive beta decay
is modified if the electron neutrino has a non-zero
mass. The unseen neutrinos are emitted uniformly in
momentum, but for a massive neutrino the change in
energy for momenta up to about $0.5*m*c$ is small, so a
relatively large number of electrons are emitted at close
to the maximum energy."

blah trying too hard here rehashing argu. made stronger elsewhere

It was bad enough when we were asked to imagine
light speed and stars signaling light back to us that had
so long ago gone out. How do you measure the dark
cut, the cave, the cut-out? Non-zero mass. Unseen
neutrinos. A plummet into a future that might have
already disappeared. *sounds like modernity*

In another bar, in Salt Lake, then called the Fat
Squirrels or the Urban Lounge or "across from the
Greek place" in another bathroom with stalls with no

doors at all, let alone locks, I was accosted by a woman whose husband was a musician. His name was not written into her forehead so you couldn't exactly call it love but she told me to marry my musician, she held my arms behind my back, marched me to the toilet. That is where love is. She flushed and flushed until I forgot about my old boyfriend, the neutrino one, whose lock on his truck door was broken. She pushed me out the door into the boyfriend who was like her husband in that the music swallowed him, in that his dancing included one foot, in that at night, on the red vinyl of his GMC pickup I could see myself in his mirror and even though I didn't carve the word "Cesar" into my forehead, I did cut my name into the bench seat of that truck of that forward moving truck. There was no going back now.

The Sudbury Neutrino Observatory (SNO) will be able to detect all three types of neutrinos, and, if we are lucky enough to have a nearby supernova, SNO may be able to improve the limits on the muon and tau neutrinos. But the supernova has already happened and the measuring has already begun. The universe is heavier, more written, more full of that black inky stuff you call sky more full of blood and forehead more full of bathroom stalls and locks and knives and edges than the most powerful telescope, more red and piercing than Hubble can measure.

How much info can you hold in ur mind @ once

—

Eleven years later, that scar on the bench seat still cuts into my leg when we go four-wheeling off Highway 180 taking the back roads to the Grand Canyon. We have expanded, not just fat ways and not just children ways, but in we scribbled our names over and over ways, over the top of each other until the words we were writing became something more than light. Heavy now, not better, not worse, but as invisible and massive as any neutrino and as already always there, staving off death even as the truck barrels faster down that already-rutted road.

MICROWIND

I inch toward you, girl. I do not go with grace. I have
been putting it off, which is not the right thing to do.
You are just a baby but even when my baby, whose
name means life in Greek, hovered in the hospital,
I did not want to be hospital bound. I prefer to go.
Tubes and traches and vents are the 21st century chains
in this broken world. Still, I should have come right
away but I had just been to Tucson where the wind
was blowing, where Zoe ate 48 orange Cuties, staving
off all scurvy and also whatever diseases everyone else
came down with later that week, where my friend from
college, Misty, chopped the red bell peppers so tiny
all the pesticides disappeared, where the re-routed
Colorado sunk into the aquifer and we turned on the
hose, brought up that water, made our own canal system
in the gravel driveway, and then recycled it ourselves,
letting it soak into the ground, back into aquifer from
whence it came. I should have gone but I am not sure
how much I can help. I do not blow much more than

gulf between knowing what's best and acting accordingly

hot air and I don't like to fly. I hate the I here. I sho
have gotten on a plane.

I would go to you girl, girl in California, girl, whe
the oranges we ate in Tucson came from, where the
Colorado goes to, if I knew that my coming would
catalyze your alveoli to do their chemical work. If there
was something the smell of me could do, the slip of my
sweat commingling with the abrasive soap that would
make the CO_2 in your lungs convert out of your blood,
to pull the oxygen in, if the dust mites on my eyelashes
could make nanowork and puff air sacs open better
than the ventilator could, if the microorganisms in my
gut, keeping me as healthy as any orange Cutie, could
bounce into your stomach and train your stomach to
pull in the whole round of the world. It's like you've got
your soul stuck halfway in and halfway out and you're
choking on it, little girl. You've been womb-free for 8
weeks, girl, and your eyes are open and looking at your
mom whose eyes I won't be able to look into when I
tell you, girl, it's not the horror of death you see but
the horror of little miracles that are just not getting off
the ground. I would like to think that my impending
arrival will bump those pneuma from concrete flats into
the phenomena they are supposed to be, pneuma from
the Greek, the vital spirit; the soul. Or in Theology,
the Spirit of God; the Holy Ghost.

I will come anyway and sing a song about being
forsaken. In between the lyrics of the song, I will chant

[handwritten annotations:]

meta
self-aware, self-co[n]
ego-narcissm

boundaries
between
bodies—
porous—
ineffective

our
imagination
tricks/
tempts us
shows us
how *closely*
we can
get

alveoli: air sacs in lungs
pneuma: creative spirit of person

torn between two (daughter, friend)

words to you. An incantation that I pray will become an incarnation. In that song about flying on the wind I will sing also the word pneuma over and over again. From the Greek: *pneûma*, literally, breath, wind, akin to *pnein*, to blow, breathe. I will say to you, forget about pneumonia. I will incant to you the pneuma and, in my dreams, it will become your lungs and I will blow myself from here, so far away, to you.

But my song, like everyone who is singing to you, is made of very privileged air. Air goes in. Air goes back out. How reliable. But wind. Wind is what you need. Where does it come from? Where does it go? Wind is its own kind of miracle. Not even the Holy Ghost can blow it himself. Wind is a small miracle and what's going to save you has got to be a little thing. Smaller than you, tiny baby. The smallest thing in the world.

circularity
air
in-out
aquifer
water
conserved

→ *It's not always the Big Cure*

"Cutie"

MICROWINDMILLS

A few miles past Cameron and the bridge that takes you
over the almost-always-empty Little Colorado, there's
a house that's been under construction for as long as
I've driven Route 89 between here and the vermillion
cliffs. The face of the house is full of features, like the
cliffs toward which I drive. It's hard not to notice two-
story tall Navajos, painted flat, their photographic faces
pressed into plywood. The man wears a cowboy hat, the
woman, a bandana. I only think they're Navajo because
the house is being constructed on the reservation
and the paint is as weathered as that plywood. Lyncia
Begay, a student of mine, works at Dillards and writes
lines of poems that do so much undoing and see so
much unseeing that they suck the air out of the room.
She hates the painted bodies on the forever-under-
construction house. Because they lie, she says. There are
no two storied Navajos out on the reservation. No one
would pose that tall. No one would paint that weather.
There aren't even any two-storied houses constructed

on the reservation. On the top of the mostly mobile, one-story houses, empty tires line roofs. On mobile homes, the sheet metal roof skin is screwed only on the perimeter, not across the top of the trusses. The tires prevent roof rumbling in the high winds. Sheet metal makes its own business, reminding the house dwellers exactly where they live which is helpful because out here, in this hundred and twenty miles of crumbling red cliffs, there are no trees to let you see the wind.

What visible things (like trees) help us see the in-visible (wind)??

MICROHEMATOCRIT

It is possible that there is not one word that cannot host
a micro in front of it. The only things I can think of are
real nouns-things you can eat. I cannot eat a hematocrit
but I can micro it. Micro is the domain of the elusive,
the abstract, the plausible but not the palpable. When
does the micro ever really matter? Perhaps only when
its meaning is displaced. Microbrew. It's not that the
beer is tiny. The Micro is not Budweiser. Not Coors.
Sometimes micro is merely a correction. I do not eat
microberries, micropotatoes, microtoast, microsteak.

On a Tuesday in the fall, any fall, it doesn't matter, fall
is always dying, dying is worse than dead, and therefore,
as beautiful as fall is, winter is still not as terrifying, I
thought I was dying. There was a lump, there was a test,
an x-ray, an electrocardiogram. There was the move,
the leaving, the new air, the lack of red only yellow
aspens, brown Gambel oaks, there was only railroad and
freeway. There was only doctor after doctor and then,

is knowing something *is there* enough?

magic, alchemy

liminal

only then, larger copays and larger appointments, the kind that filled hours and required out-patient. How could I die so many ways in just one year? I held my cat close to me because he, I knew, would die before me and I could gauge my fear in the thinness of his skin, the rosary of his bones. His teeth were covered in tiny dots of red. It was not the red I had been missing. I missed his large orange fur. The markings that made him look like an ocelot. I missed the things I could see.

anthropo,
cat

nine
lives

micro-
macroscopic

MICROSOCCER

I tried to bring a book. I tried to bring a chair. I tried
to talk to the other moms. I tried to talk to the dads.
I tried to bring the team snack but failed, bringing
carrots. I tried to get a sense that you can kick the
ball first if you're the one who kicked it off but I
think I have that wrong too. I tried to pull the grass
and eat the milky ends but there was elk shit all over
and dog piss probably too. Really, there was nothing
to eat except carrots and therefore, I had a hard
time paying attention. She didn't kick the ball hard
enough and when she did kick it, the ball went out of
bounds. Sometimes, she kicked it the wrong direction.
Sometimes, someone kicked it hard, in the wrong
direction and all the kids ran all the way out of bounds,
offsides, down the hill, over elk shit and dog piss chasing
a ball that would never come back. For me, it was good
for a metaphor anyway—chasing youth or boys or of
hungry members of the *Cervidae* family looking for
edible grass on the other side of the mountain where

[handwritten margin notes:]
sun on horizon line
field animals
motherhood spectator in the shitty weeds
grass always greener
→ deer

perhaps the fire or the drought didn't wipe out all the grass.

I apologized. I needed to apply some kind of drama because I wasn't going to get up off my chair or put down my book and join them in chasing that ball. I knew I'd never catch it and the team would never forgive me for getting in the way of a game whose rules have nothing to do with how to get fed.

mother,
nurturer
"soccer mom"

MICROBLOGS

Because *Scientific American* reports a study that found
that people recall Facebook status updates more readily
than they recall information read from a book. Because
Scientific American calls Facebook posts Microblogs.
Because microblogs resemble ordinary speech.
Because microblogs say what you mean and don't try
to be fancy. Because there is already someone to listen.
Because the world "sepulcher" is never used. Because
books are sepulchers. Because the word "shimmering,"
a word often used in book so poetry is rarely used
in status updates and if it is so used, it is easy
to unfriend the user. Because the politics are already
agreed upon. Because the cadence is the cadence of
early humans. Because the early humans communicated
contextually. Because the context is a face. Because a
face is easy to remember. Because a friend is someone
who says things you like. Although the scientists didn't
think humans would remember words written in such
haste. Because the scientists are often surprised. Because

[handwritten margin note:] * this is huge for the magic of the internet — the assurance you'll be heard

[handwritten note at bottom left:] simplified, dumbed down

[handwritten note at bottom center:] algorithms v. primal instinct, habit

what is more important than something written in haste, without care, but to someone who will read it. Because teachers might incorporate this into their lessons. Because students are early humans too. Because I will teach a class on because my students would like class to read a microblog full of context and care and faces. Because the world needs more faces. Because the world needs more, if shorter, words. Because I can remember what you said in your last Facebook post about those with the smallest hearts have the greatest freedom although I can't remember who posted it and although I can't remember what famous writer said it first but I can remember each of the words in the exact right order which is more than I can say about anything I wrote except maybe the one day I wrote a Facebook post about being so tired I wanted to put my head in a bucket of sleep and the words were well-liked and I was well-liked and I went into the day tired but finally, for what seemed like the first time, read. And, according to *Scientific American,* my Facebook friends will indeed remember about sleep and buckets but you, reader, will not remember this essay because it is longer than the accepted word length of a microblog and it is full of long sentences and words I don't even remember. Because neither you nor I will remember who wrote the article in the *Scientific American* or who did the research or who invented Facebook but I will remember to friend you when I get home so I can begin to remember you.

Handwritten marginalia:

What does it mean to be an "early human"? just starting out learning this craft, this world, this way of being

tiny tuthers of dopamine can actually mean a lot

friend, like, retweet

the schema, physical-literal-genre structures + how they affect our interpretation/reading and memory

MICROFIRE

It started small. Not two kids with rubbing sticks.
Not two members from the Nation setting pranks
behind dumpsters. Not two ATV riders with very
sunburnt necks sparking their batteries. Not two
hippies who spaced putting sand on their fire. Not even
overachieving squirrels. Not ravens with a match. No
there was no direct cause for this fire that is burning
over 7000 acres for this fire that is the Bambi Disney
version, forcing squirrels and skunks and raccoons to
flee and is also not Disney-like in that humans evacuate
their fire-magnetic homes and shelter at the Yavapai
Community Center. Take refuge. Get away.

   Evacuations are not all that rare. Last year, the big
fire out by Payson, and two years ago, the Wallow
fire, largest fire in Arizona history, and three years ago
the Schultz fire and then also the one that had our
housesitter packing up her car with all the pictures she
could find of our kids and the pictures that our kids had
drawn and the things that looked like important pieces

[handwritten annotation:] → abandoning post
— the house rock seems
   to be disintegrating, dividing,
                                 abandoning

of paper, drawn by the kids or not, as she frantically
tried to call us as we camped so naively out by Sycamore
Point just thirteen miles away but too far for cell service
and too far to know that the fire called Little America
was turning toward our house and the winds were
up and the humidity low and in June in Arizona you
should know better and keep a pack of memorabilia
packed and ready to go because you are human and you
will forget everything that you ever learned without a
piece of paper on which to write it down.

fallibility

You had better treasure that paper. The trees. They
are burning down. The trees, some say, will not come
back. The trees need certain conditions. Some humidity.
Some rain. Some days where temperatures are below 32
degrees. Other plants may grow. Juniper and chaparral.
Pinyon Pine. Maybe we can make paper out of juniper
upon which we can invest our memories and protect
them from a fire that is coming since fires like that just
aren't that rare anymore.

*paper-
trees-
karmic*

*ironic-
writing
about
blazed
trees*

In Prescott, no one is blaming anyone directly for
the 19 firefighters who died. At the Yavapai Community
Center, a man sits on the edge of his cot. Another man
stands a couple of miles away, white lines through black
ash. In the Center, a woman quiets her baby. The baby
is hot and the corner seems the coolest, quietest space.
Back at the fire, a woman digs her Hotshot shovel into
the ground. Fire lines. They used to work. Maybe they
will work today. There is another man, a fire detective,

walking the line between forest and the Center. In
between, he will find the cause, but never a direct one.
Human-caused for sure. All the fires now. Just touch the
air. Touch the ground. It hasn't rained for months now.
The humans are good at so many things: starting fires
and stopping rain.

aphorisms get at our
animal + superhuman
capacities, both

MICROTOPOGRAPHY

When I was thirteen, my boyfriend's mother used to
drive us to Sugarhouse Park. At Sugarhouse Park, she
would sit us next to the rocks by the river. The river
came from the mountains. The river came over the
rocks. The rocks made the river flow hard. The rocks
gave the river what gravity and slope couldn't. Bubbles.
My boyfriend's mother made us sit by the bubbles to
inhale the negative ions that she promised would make
us happy. We sat by the river as it rushed and as it
bubbled. We breathed in the bubbles, happily. On the
ride home, my boyfriend drove. I sat in the in middle.
His mother sat to my right. I held a bag of Doritos
between my legs. He fished for chips. He fished with
his finger. His eyes looked straight ahead but his finger
never stopped. His mother told us about a river too far
away where the water fell fifty feet straight down. The
whole canyon was full of ions, negative ones, looking
for some positive ion to catch itself onto, to tickle its
magnet, to pull the whole fabric closer to its edge,

[handwritten marginalia: how is everything knit together / skein writing / sexual fingering (between) mother + son / mother nature / "saving," inoculating / vectors, pinballing energy in car / orgasm]

to threaten to punch through the plastic and make
something purely invented, real.

fantasy/reality
limits of eyesight
  ↳that's where
  language takes up the work

MICROMEMORY

The starling had broken his wing. It was just a starling but even a starling looks beautiful when it's bouncing on two legs, looking for flight. Will had had a long day. He found out his mother was dying. She would be taken to hospice that very afternoon. The cancer ate her throat. And then her lymph nodes. And then it started nibbling on her brain. Will kept trying to remember his mother when she was young and healthy but he could not bring a single picture of her into his mind. He could see her piano but not hear her play. He knew she made layered cakes but he couldn't remember what flavor. His mother was already gone but he still had to go sit with her at her hospice bed and talk as if all talk wasn't about the future.

He put on some work gloves, walked over to the starling. He thought at first of putting the bird out of its misery but he could only kill so many things off in one day. He picked up the bird, put it in a shoebox. He drove to the aviary where he hoped they could cure

our human search for beauty, clarity, resolution, logic,

small ugly things that sometimes look beautiful when
there's nothing else to look at.   *cause + effect*

MICROISLAND

Margie and I were talking about the weather. It was raining at five in the afternoon. "My friend, Fredricka, who lives next store and who has been here thirty years, said during monsoon, it would rain like clockwork from one until three and then you could go about your business. Now, you can't tell when a storm is coming."

"It's happening everywhere. In Iowa, summer is so long now," Margie says. Margie is from Manila. She says her friends in the Philippines don't care about climate change. "These are people on an Island! They're going to get sunk first." We laughed. Possibly nervously. She told me about a tiny island she visits every couple of years. A four-hundred year old Balete tree sits in the middle of the island. When Margie was young, her family would come for picnics and to swim and to sit under the long arms of the Balete. Now, the water is up to the roots of the tree. Soon, the salt water will erode the roots and the tree will fall down. "I take people there to see it. I say, look, there goes our tree." But they don't see it. Not

even as it sinks right before their eyes. Maybe they think
their own islands will be lifted up in some kind of scales
of justice kind of balance. Maybe all our feet are getting
wet and we stand around and blame the sand for not
being sturdier.

we avoid, at
all costs, the
really hard truths

MICROSPIKES

Janice Romick is a saver of the bees. She plants lavender,
mint, and sunflowers around the hexagonal patio of her
condominium. She would plant artichokes, if they could
grow well around a patio in Utah, so she could see the
bees tumble upside down in the overgrown thistle. She
loves to imagine the comfort the needly purple petals
provide to needled bee bodies. She's stopped using
Roundup on the dandelions that grown in the patio's
cracks. Stopped making calls on her cell phone. She has
done everything she can think to stop disrupting the bee
colonies but she knows she is just one and there are too
many disruptions to try to think about the bees every
day, anyway.

Inside her house, a yellow jacket bounces against
the window shaped like a hexagon that looks from
the inside out to the yard. The yellow jacket slides up
the glass and down until she's certain it can't make its
way out on its own. She picks up a paper napkin—the
cheap, not even recycled kind—and approaches the

empathy for the teensy

our incongruities, fallibilities

yellow jacket fast and confident, pinching it with her fingers. Not too hard. Gently. She lifts the napkin, opens the door that leads to the patio and lets the yellow jacket free into the relative safety of the mint.

She does this a lot. She's been stung a few times. She's not sure why the yellow jackets persist in coming into her house. Perhaps they plan to colonize her home, her house a hexagon, her house of windows, her house of doors that does good work to keep the disruptions out. She thinks she can probably get along with them just fine as long as she doesn't bother them or they her. But that's the hard thing. Figuring out which of you is the poked and which the poker. What is the inside of the giant honeycomb is and what is the out.

harmony can
sometimes resemble
separation

MICROBAGS

At Fry's Grocery and Drugstore, the plastic bags are
tinted brown. Thin enough to see through, they should
be strong enough to hold at least three items. But the
clerks at Fry's dig their hands into the abundance of
bags. Stacked like money, peeled like sawbucks, a bag
wraps a carton of eggs. Another, a half gallon of orange
juice. Another, a pound of butter. Another, a quart of
milk. A loaf of bread. You know the song. Each bag
makes each item precious. How can I eat this butter
now? I should preserve it in a cabinet of wonder but
by the time I get home the cabinet of wonder becomes
merely a refrigerator. The loaf of bread. The quart of
milk. Each item reshelved in the icebox of my future—I
now can make béchamel, French Toast, crème Anglaise,
Pasta Carbonara, countries of recipes, thanks to bags of
permanence and transportation.

The bags, emptied, do not realign. I cannot stack
them. They do not fit in my billfold. I bunch them
up. I crush them into the reusable canvas bags that I

should
↑ *be GARBAGE*

sometimes remember to take to the store. The bags
live in the garage. Unlike the refrigerator, the garage is
not airtight. Sometimes, I leave the garage door open.
Sometimes, there is a wind. Sometimes the wind comes
in and steals the plastic bags as if the wind had some
groceries to make precious. The wind takes the bags,
plasters them against Ponderosa, wraps them around
pinecone, flags them against a decaying stick. The stick *infection,*
isn't going anywhere now. The Ponderosas preserved. *sickness*
The pinecones, seeding inside of the bag, with the
benefit of a dusty rain, grow their own tree inside the *condom*
bag. Inside the bag is a perfect microcosm. A hundred
million tiny planets floating across the state, blowing
their forevers across the highway, through the forests,
across the ocean, establishing themselves as normal as
continental cash.

*there's a lot of
gross sad poetic
beauty in climatic
change
—images*

*best captured
in aphorism*

MICROAPOCALYPSE

I only have one friend, Steve, who thinks we will
survive the apocalypse. I stockpile jarred tomatoes.
He stockpiles guns. We will need each other and have
to find a way to traverse the 500 miles that separates
us. We will also need: sourdough starter made from
wretched old grapes fermenting in yet another Mason
jar; one of those newfangled straws that filters water
even when you stick it into a nearly toxic cesspool; one
cow or goat for milk, two chickens for eggs, a solar-
powered automobile that can hold at least a family of
four, a goat, sun, limes, avocado, salt. We will not need
to reinvent the wheel or electricity. We may need to
reinvent the Internet and flush toilets. We will need
scissors, papers, pens, paperclips, staples—general
office supplies—because if there is one thing we will
surely miss, it is rebuilding the tax-code. Benjamin
Franklin said it was the library, or possibly fire stations,
that made a civilization, but if there is one thing that
unites us all, it is our love of April 15th. Shared goals.

A catholic expectation. We will need seeds from not
Monsanto and heart medication not from Merck. We
will need the old growth forest back. We will need the
polar bear back. We will need that one frog who keeps
changing his sex back and forth depending on how
much Prozac is in the water to finally pick a team and
stick with it. We will need an ocean full of fish and
oysters who forgot the name red tide. We will need
someone to make movies and someone to critique them.
We may need books but possibly only ones that have
nice things to say about fish. We will need to partner
with the otters to learn how to stay warm in the winter
and to discuss with the prairie dogs how to make a
proper communal town where all the berries are good
for all the dogs, prairie or not. We will need not only
jarred tomatoes but lemon curd. We will need apple pie.
We will need to learn to make béchamel with milk from
our friend, the goat. We will need someone who knows
how to make guitars and someone who knows how
to play one. We will need a blanket, a square sewn by
everyone who ever thought, man, this might be the end
and then, wakes up the next day, happy that it isn't. In
the end, we will need a lot of things but I think it's going
to be OK because these days, Mason jars are plentiful
and everyone I know is named Steve.

[handwritten annotations: "hermaphroditism"; "always conscious of the flip side, the 'other'"; "call back to previous"]

ACKNOWLEDGMENTS

"House of Bees," *Orion*
"Neutrinos," *Menagerie*
"Microblogs," *The Journal of Microliterature*
"Microbags," "Microchip," "Microtrain," and
    "Microsoccer," *The Account*
"Microbivalves," "Microbiotics," and "Microapocalypse,"
    Terrain.org
"Dear Galaxy" and "Dear Wind," *Hotel Amerika*
"Microencephaly," *Sweet*
"Microhematocrit" and "Microhabitat," *The Collagist*
"Microsurgery," *5X5*

Several of the microessays here were published as
    part of a longer essay, "Distracted Parents of the
    Micromanagement Era," in *Black Warrior Review*

The Edward Wright quotation on page 37 is from
<http://www.astro.ucla.edu/~wright/neutrinos.html>.

NICOLE WALKER's forthcoming books include *Processed Meats* from Atticus Press in late 2016 and *Egg* from Bloomsbury in 2017. Her collection of essays, *Quench Your Thirst with Salt*, won the Zone 3 Press Award for Creative Nonfiction. *This Noisy Egg*, a collection of poems, was published by Barrow Street in 2010. She edited, with Margot Singer, *Bending Genre: Essays on Creative Nonfiction*, published by Bloomsbury. A recipient of a fellowship from the NEA, she's nonfiction editor at *DIAGRAM* and Associate Professor at Northern Arizona University in Flagstaff, Arizona where it rains like the Pacific Northwest, but only in July.

❋

COLOPHON

Text is set in a digital version of Jenson, designed by Robert Slimbach in 1996, and based on the work of punchcutter, printer, and publisher Nicolas Jenson. The titles here are in Futura.

✺

NEW MICHIGAN PRESS, based in Tucson, Arizona, prints poetry and prose chapbooks, especially work that transcends traditional genre. Together with DIAGRAM, NMP sponsors a yearly chapbook competition.

DIAGRAM, a journal of text, art, and schematic, is published bimonthly at THEDIAGRAM.COM. Periodic print anthologies are available from the New Michigan Press at NEWMICHIGANPRESS.COM.

CPSIA information can be obtained
at www.ICGtesting.com
Printed in the USA
LVHW040012211218
601322LV00001B/26/P